Kingdom Publishing Presents

God Met Me Here 2

Kingdom Publishing Presents

God Met Me Here 2

Stories of how God shows up in everyday life.

KINGDOM
PUBLISHING

We would like to acknowledge the following individuals for permission to print the following material.

I Want a Story. Reprinted by permission of Charity Ruch © 2022 Charity Ruch.

He Sat with Me. Reprinted by permission of Traci Robinson © 2022 Traci Robinson.

In the Middle of Nowhere. Reprinted by permission of Karen Crowfoot © 2022 Karen Crowfoot.

Hilarious Healing. Reprinted by permission of B D Johnson © 2022 B D Johnson.

My Love Story: Spirit, Soul and Body. Reprinted by permission of Rebekah Lind © 2022 Rebekah Lind.

A Miracle in Alaska During the Pandemic. Reprinted by permission of Constance Kay Thompson © 2022 Constance Kay Thompson.

November 1977. Reprinted by permission of Sharon Burrell © 2022 Sharon Burrell.

Co-Parenting with God. Reprinted by permission of Tracy Fagan © 2022 Tracy Fagan.

How God Met Me in the Depth of My Fear. Reprinted by permission of Michael Blaes © 2022 Michael Blaes.

One Day Does Matter. Reprinted by permission of Daniel Fariss © 2022 Daniel Fariss.

Cover Design: Tracy Fagan

ISBN 978-1-7375156-6-1 (paperback)

ISBN 978-1-7375156-7-8 (ebook)

Table of Contents

Introduction

Welcome to *God Met Me Here 2*. I've always been a sucker for God stories. Sometimes people categorize them as "big God stories" or "little God stories"; from my perspective, anytime the God of the universe chooses to personally interact with someone, that is a big God story.

The fact this book made its way into your hands is no coincidence. One of the ways God encourages people is through the stories of the things He has done. Through these stories, we come to understand who God is and how He rolls. Take a look at the Bible. There are many amazing stories of how God delivered people out of bondage, blessed individuals, and fought and won battles for those who loved Him.

Before we go any further, I want to address another truth.

God loves you dearly.

It doesn't matter if you speak with Him every day, if you had a relationship with God and walked away, or have never known Him; God will never love you any more or any less than He does right now. His love is incomprehensible.

From my own personal experience, I have to say it took me a while to believe God really loves me. I still have trouble sometimes receiving all He has for me. I share that with you so you don't get stuck in the pattern of beating yourself up because you don't "feel" God's love.

Through the pages of this book, I believe He is going to begin to reveal His love story for you. He tells us in His Word that He shows no favoritism. (Romans 2:11) If you begin saying to yourself things like, "but I'm not good enough," or "but you don't know what I have done;" tell the voices in your head to be quiet. Every last one of us has sinned and fallen short of the glory of God. That is why His love for us is so scandalous.

Let me step back for a moment. If you have never had a relationship with God, or if you had one that has faded, I would ask you to keep an open mind as you read the stories in this book. Instead of saying, "There is no way that can be true," come with the mindset, "If that really is true, God, please help me believe!" If you have just an ever-so-tiny amount of faith that God just might be real, and you ask Him to reveal Himself to you, He will. That is one of the promises He gives us in His Word. (Matthew 7:8)

As you dive into these amazing stories, keep in mind, some of these authors had a close relationship with God at the time when He met them. Some authors had walked away from their relationship with Him, while others had never known God personally. I point this out to let you know that no matter which category you find yourself, God wants to meet you right where you are. He already knows you, and loves you. He is reaching out because He wants to be in relationship with you.

God reminds us several times in His Word that He will never leave us nor forsake us. In other words, He is ALWAYS with us. However, in each of our lives, we can look back and find specific times when He met us right there, in that moment! It is those times when you sit there in amazement with what just happened...or didn't happen. And there is no other explanation...except God.

God gave me the inspiration to gather these stories and create this series of books through an experience where He personally met me...at the intersection of Potomac Street and Broncos Parkway in Centennial, Colorado.

My daughter and I were leaving Bible study. She was driving home, and we were about ½ mile from the church. She was getting ready to turn left - and she had the green arrow. As she started to go, God brought to my attention a car that was driving towards the intersection at full speed. I then saw a brief vision of a horrific accident. Out of my mouth came the stern command, "STOP!" My daughter reacted immediately. The black SUV came barreling through his red light and not hitting his brakes until after he was all the way through the intersection. Immediately, I knew that God had saved our lives. When thanking God for what He had done, I heard Him say, "Tracy, I met you here; right at the corner of Potomac Street and Broncos Parkway."

When God meets people, it isn't always through a drastic, life-saving situation. Sometimes it is through simple small signs or nudges. For example, when I was in a very toxic relationship, trying to find peace, I would retreat to the back deck, close my eyes, and bask warmth of the sun. When I would go out there, I heard this "hmmmmmm…vrooommmmmm" sound. When I opened my eyes, I saw hummingbirds hovering in mid-air and then diving down. The visual show and the accompanying sound effects put a smile on my face and brought me comfort. When I left that relationship and moved into my own place, I hung a hummingbird feeder from my balcony. On the spring mornings, I would lay in bed and find comfort watching and hearing these beautiful little creatures come and feast. It seems as though these unique birds are sent by God to me to bring peace. I love how their unique sound will alert me to their presence.

God is intentional. I don't believe in coincidences. I encourage you to think about an encounter, a pattern, or a person who came at "just the right time." Could that be God meeting you right where you are?

In the stories that follow, you will begin to gain an understanding of who God is and how He protects and leads us through different situations and circumstances. Notice He doesn't always take the situations or circumstances away, but will meet you right where you are to help you navigate through the trial. Even in His Word

He tells us that we will experience trouble in this world. Jesus promises us His peace because He has overcome the world. (John 16:33)

As you read the stories in this book, keep in mind God placed this book in your hands for a reason. I believe it's because He wants a personal relationship with you. To learn more about what this means and how to begin this relationship, go to page 69. There, I will share with you more about what it means to be saved, as well as share a prayer with you that will ask Jesus into your heart.

For now, I invite you to jump in and be encouraged as you read these stories of our amazing God and His love for His children.

I Want a Story
Charity Ruch

"I want a story."

These are the words that came out of my mouth one January evening. One of my best friends had invited me to a MOPS meeting where a comedian was speaking on how to be happy when life is messy. I laughed because I had seen so many challenges in my life over the last several years that there was no way some speaker was going to teach me any lessons on this. In fact, I had spent the last two years in weekly therapy trying to find a glimmer of happiness in my mess. Even though my expectations for the evening were low, I had a one-, four-, and six-year-old at home so I wasn't going to say no to a couple of hours of adult interaction.

The speaker talked about some really tough things in her life; a failed marriage, job loss, health struggles, and some near-death experiences. However, I kind of glossed over her hardships because I had just survived the worst possible season of life I could have imagined, including almost dying.

When my oldest daughter was born, we both had lots of complications during delivery and I ended up with severe postpartum hemorrhaging. I passed out and when I came to, the nurse was telling me that I wasn't going to feel very well because I had just lost over half my blood. I was so sick; I didn't even remember I had a baby! It took me a while to comprehend what happened, but apparently when they couldn't get the bleeding to stop, they prepared the operating room for a full hysterectomy. As they were getting ready to wheel my bed into surgery, the bleeding miraculously stopped. They were able to stabilize me with a handful of blood transfusions and lots of medications. I almost died that day, and I wasn't the only one fighting to live.

My daughter experienced life-threatening issues of her own. She had a high fever, was positioned the wrong way during delivery, and the umbilical cord was wrapped around her neck. The doctors and nurses had a hard time stabilizing her heart rate from her stressful entrance into the world, and they whisked her away before I even had the chance to meet her.

The fact we were both alive and had no long-term damage was a miracle. I went from fully enjoying my life to not taking a single second for granted. I was overwhelmed with gratitude every single moment of every single day. Laundry, dishes, sleepless nights, early mornings, all of it. I was so grateful and thankful that I got to live and see my daughter grow up. Little did I know that my new-found zest for life would quickly be taken away.

When my third baby was born, I had a complication from delivery that left me with unexplained nerve damage in my leg. I mentioned it at the hospital, but they told me everything was fine and sent me home. But my leg didn't work; it was basically paralyzed. I could not drive because there wasn't enough muscle to push on the brake pedal or keep constant pressure on the gas. I struggled to walk, and get up and down from the floor. I couldn't kick off my shoes or cross my legs. How do you navigate those waters when you have a newborn and two other young children to care for? This all led to extremely severe anxiety and depression that put me in the emergency room multiple times. To be honest, I literally have no memory of the first six months of her life. All I remember is going to doctor after doctor, begging someone to help me. I cried out to God in desperation every minute of every day, begging Him to heal me. I pleaded and bargained with Him; I yelled at Him and unleashed all my anger up to Heaven. I felt like my life was over.

Although no one knew at the time, my leg issue was not permanent. It grew stronger and stronger, and I was finally able to function again. Before I even had a chance to fully realize God was healing my leg, another trauma reared its ugly head. I was so focused on trying to keep my head above water, I glazed over the fact that my only prayer request for so long was for my leg to work again.

One day, my kids were playing and begging me to go down the slide with them. I finally agreed because I was trying to "be present in the moment" like my therapist had been urging me to do. So, I got off the sidelines and joined my kids; but the second I hit the bottom of the slide, I immediately knew something was wrong. I badly hurt my tailbone and I panicked. Days of constant pain turned into weeks, which turned into months. Everyone kept telling me to give it time and not to worry. But a year later, despite tons of doctor appointments, it still wasn't any better, and sitting was incredibly painful. I was told it was going to be like this forever, and that there was nothing anyone could do.

This was my background as I walked into the MOPS group to hear that speaker talk about her "hard life." I listened to the whole thing, unimpressed with her story because I felt I was dealing with a much harder version. Towards the end, I don't remember exactly what she said, but it must have been something to the effect of "this is my story." Because I immediately turned to my friend and said-

"I want a story."

I regretted saying this at the exact time the words were coming out of my mouth. It felt like I had just accidentally unlocked Pandora's box, and I wasn't even interested in opening it in the first place.

My friend who had been with me through every single hardship over the past few years looked at me like I was actively growing a second head and said, "You already have a story!"

She was right. I already had a story. A big, messy story full of grief and loss and heartache. That was my story, and no, I didn't want another one. I'm pretty sure if I had been listening hard enough, I would have heard God laughing. I didn't know it at the time, but my story was just getting started.

I had been dealing with some pain in my chest and along my ribs. I figured I just pulled a muscle, but I went to the doctor anyway because it wasn't getting better.

He told me everything was fine and sent me home with some muscle relaxers. Hours later, the ache turned into the worst pain I'd ever experienced. The doctor ordered a CT scan that showed I had a large blood clot in my lung. It had stopped the blood from circulating and caused part of my lung to die. (The medical term for this is pulmonary embolism, or PE, with a lung infarction.) I spent several days in the hospital in unimaginable pain. Doctors and nurses said I was lucky to be alive, and that many times a PE is discovered during an autopsy.

Little did I know, this was just the opening act of what would become the hardest season of my life. So many things happened in a short period of time, it became a checklist of traumatic events: falling down the stairs, three deaths in the family, disease diagnoses, surgeries, and broken bones just to name a few. I was completely overwhelmed.

On May 7, 2019, I was at the hospital saying goodbye to my sweet nephew who had passed away the day before. I left the hospital to go pick up my oldest from STEM School in Highlands Ranch, Colorado. As I was driving, my friend who lives nearby sent me a text saying something was happening. Emergency vehicles started racing past me and I immediately knew something was wrong. I received her text that said "shooting" at the same time I turned into the school to see the place swarming with police cars. I was living every parent's worst nightmare. There was an active shooter at my baby's school and she was trapped inside. It was complete chaos and no one knew what was going on. Worst of all, there was not a single thing I could do to help her. That day my mama heart felt pain like it had never felt before.

They sent everyone to a nearby recreation center to await further instruction. The phone lines were overloaded and I couldn't send or receive any texts or calls. After a while, there was chatter that something had happened in the high school portion of the building, but no one knew exactly what. I prayed that meant my first grader was OK. I clung to that because it was my only lifeline.

A few hours later, I saw her class walking toward the rec center. They were all holding hands and walking in a single file line. As soon as I saw her face, I was completely overwhelmed with emotion. She was fine, but many others were not. A young man named Kendrick Castillo died saving his classmates from two gunmen. A dozen others were injured. I felt like school was not a safe place for my kids to be anymore. I was a wreck.

I couldn't take it anymore. The world was cruel. Everything happening in my life was just too much to handle. The verse I had clung to all these years seemed empty. *The LORD is close to the brokenhearted and saves those who are crushed in spirit.* (Psalm 34:18 NIV) God wasn't anywhere to be found, much less near me. My heart was broken into four million pieces. Saying my spirit was crushed was an understatement.

I was in a constant daze. It was like I was always looking through a foggy window. I was experiencing life, but I was missing all the details and emotions that make life worth living. I was angry, bitter, hurt, and resentful. I was only in my 30's; I was too young for all this to be happening. I turned to one of my friends and unleashed my anger. Why was God allowing all this to happen? He's not around. He doesn't even see me. He's sitting up there on his throne letting me suffer. I told her I felt like God had completely abandoned me.

That's when she said this:

"God has met you in so many places! Think about it. You are alive despite many attempts to the contrary. And He has healed and protected you in so many ways."

I didn't want to hear it at first, but as I let her words sink in, it was like someone opened a door and allowed me to see all the miracles in my life lined up in a row. How did I miss them all? My friend was right; it was so obvious. God had met me each and every time something happened, and I was just beginning to realize it.

My story could have easily ended multiple times, but it didn't. God met me in the mess. And while He didn't answer all of my prayers like I wanted Him to, He DID answer some of them—and they were big ones. He healed my leg, stopped my bleeding, protected my daughter, and allowed me to live— twice!

I couldn't believe I had so easily glossed over His goodness so many times. He took off my blinders and showed me that there is beauty in the ashes. It's a good thing when I'm poor in faith, He's rich in love because it's easy to miss His mercies when I'm in the middle of a mess.

So, it turns out, I do have a story.

Except, I don't want my story to be circumstantial. I want it to be a testament to His power and everlasting love; a story that makes others open up their hearts to God because it can't be explained any other way. I want it to bring glory to Him, even when I feel like I'm drowning in grief and sorrow. I have to trust Him when it seems like my pleas for healing fall short of Heaven. There's no denying He has His hand on my life, and He's writing my story according to His will.

I don't know how many times He's going to need to teach me this same lesson, but when life feels impossible and like it's too much to handle, He will meet me in the mess— every single time.

Charity Ruch

Charity lives in Highlands Ranch, Colorado with her husband and three children. She fell in love with writing at a very young age and believes nothing is more powerful than stories that linger on your heart long after you've read them.

She graduated with a degree in journalism, and spent the next ten years writing and producing shows for popular television networks including *HGTV, Discovery Channel, Food Network* and *RFD-TV*. This work took her to nearly all fifty states and allowed her to tell stories about people from all walks of life.

After nearly dying and dealing with a laundry list of traumatic events, she started a blog called, *Little Ones, Big Things*. Here she shares deeply personal stories and details about her faith, tough experiences and health struggles. Her hope is she can help support others who are navigating through life's storms so they never have to feel alone.

Charity loves hiking in the beautiful Rocky Mountains and spending time with her friends and family. She enjoys doing crafts and food art of all kinds, which she also features on her blog.

🌐 littleonesbigthings.com
f @littleonesbigthings
📷 @littleones_bigthings
📌 @LittleOnes_BigThings

He Sat with Me
Traci Robinson

A nxious for results and disoriented in the cramped room of the pregnancy center, I jumped at the nurse's report. "It's positive, you're pregnant." She paused, then continued, "What are you leaning toward doing?" Confusion rippled through me. I had no idea. I didn't know what my options were. I'd never been here before. Impatient with my delay, she shoved papers at me and sent me on my way.

A few days later, when I called to make the appointment, I felt ashamed and wondered what the woman on the other end of the phone might ask. Surprisingly, she didn't ask much, just made the appointment and instructed me where to go. I expected relief as I hung up. It didn't come.

The day before the appointment, I canceled. I couldn't go through with the abortion. This time, as I hung up the phone, I found that sense of relief I had been looking for.

That night, lying on the floor of my childhood bedroom with a child growing inside me, I prayed. I hadn't prayed in years. I'd spent my teens running from God, not talking with Him. That night, I asked what He wanted me to do. That's when Jesus took the lead.

A bright yellow flyer pinned to the bulletin board at my after-school job the next day boasted the answer to my prayer. That flyer wasn't there the day before.

There hadn't been anything on that board the entire year I worked there. This day was different.

The flyer was advertising a local Christian adoption agency. I knew it was for me. I knew it was the way Jesus was leading me. I called the number.

Dialing, I was just as nervous as when I'd called the abortion clinic, but after making the appointment at the adoption agency, I didn't feel as alone. I had peace. While I still didn't know what to do, I knew I'd just connected with someone who did.

The first time I met with the counselor, she was stunned by the fact I was so sure about my decision that early in the pregnancy. She told me I needed to take more time. I assured her I didn't need it. I'd been shown the yellow flyer; I knew what I needed to do.

After several weeks we met again. This time it was at a restaurant. I'll never forget, I ate the Cobb chicken salad. It's funny the things that stick with you when you're facing decisions you never imagined you would.

She brought several portfolios of families with her. I looked through them with excitement and hope; and ever so carefully. As I turned the last page of the last one, a wave of disappointment and panic came over me. The family I was looking for wasn't there. I knew it. What was I going to do? I was so sure this was what God wanted for me and for the child I carried.

The next time we met, she had new portfolios. Families had been added because they were either new to the adoption agency or put back into the group because another young woman changed her mind about adoption. I was hopeful and curious. It's a strange thing flipping pages in search of a family for your child. What do you look for? How do you know? Again, Jesus led.

It was important to me that the family had already adopted a child so that my child would have a sibling they could share his or her story with and hopefully find a place of understanding and belonging. While pouring over the pages, the cutest boy caught my eye and instantly captured my heart. I just knew he would be the best older brother. Closing the book, I sighed and smiled as happy tears welled up. I wanted to meet them!

The mom was fun, her laugh filled the room. Quiet but friendly, the dad's steadiness proved calming for all of us. I knew they weren't perfect—no family is—but they were perfect for me, for my baby. They were the ones I'd been looking for!

Months later, while working through so many emotions as I settled into knowing this baby would not be coming home with me, I scribbled in a school notebook:

Love:

Sometimes love isn't what's expected.

Sometimes love isn't acknowledged or recognized.

Usually love is expressed with flowers, letters, hugs, and kisses.

Very rarely is love expressed with a good-bye.

Good-bye, little one. Good-bye.

I wish all the best for you.

I will never forget your eyes.

I love you more than you or anyone will ever know.

You will never fully understand why I let you go

Good-bye, little one. Good-bye.

The time we spent together you won't remember, but I hope somewhere deep down you'll remember my voice and the words I said to you.

I love you.

It is so hard to let you go, but it really is the best thing for you.

Tomorrow will bring new light.

You won't understand all this tonight but maybe in time.

Good-bye, little one. Good-bye.

Barely poetic, it expressed my raw emotions. Jesus was making me ready.

Months passed. Then, finally, the day came. It was time.

The adoptive parents spent hours in the hospital waiting room. They sent in a cute card and a beautiful bouquet of white roses. The baby arrived in the very early morning. It was a girl! I'll never forget the first time I saw her. Beautiful. Perfect. Healthy. A precious gift from God.

The adoptive parents wanted to meet her right away. I wasn't quite ready. I requested that they go home. It must have been scary thinking I might have been having second thoughts. I wasn't. I just needed some time.

After a while, everyone left—the adoptive parents, my parents, my friend, the doctors, and nurses. The baby was in the nursery. I was alone in the hospital room, or so I thought. I brushed my teeth and washed my face. Looking deep into my eyes in my reflection in the mirror, my heart asked, "Am I being true to myself, to my daughter, to God? Will I be able to face myself tomorrow and in the future? Will I be able to face my daughter?"

I thought I was alone; but in fact, I wasn't. After those questions poured from my heart, I immediately felt the presence of Jesus like never before. It was as if He was sitting on my bed, just being with me.

He sat with me.

That was all the answer I needed.

The following morning, the adoptive family came to meet their newest family member. The adoptive mom walked in, looked at her new baby girl, and said, "Hi, Kate!" It was bittersweet for me, my heart breaking and jumping for joy in the same moment.

Later that afternoon, the adoption counselor tenderly asked me, "Are you ready?"

I took a deep breath and responded, "Almost. Is it okay if I take a few minutes alone with Kate?"

"Of course!"

I held my daughter cheek to cheek, kissed her again and again. Weeping, I prayed aloud, barely able to get words out: "I'm giving her back to you. I'm giving her back to you."

I trusted Him. He handpicked her family. He knew her story. He was writing it. I just had to follow His lead, even though it hurt.

After those moments, I was ready. It was time for her to go home.

Placing her into her mom's arms, I pictured Jesus holding the new mom as she held her baby girl. I was confident He would lead them just as He had led us here from that bedroom floor prayer months earlier.

The ride home was like nothing else. It wasn't just the baby who had grown over the past several months; I had grown too. We had grown together. Now we were apart. I felt a deep ache and sense of loss. But a sense of pride roared slightly louder than the loss. I knew my daughter now had something I was unable to give her: a stable, intact family chosen by the Lord. Sitting in the backseat of my parents' car, I felt the tears streaming down my face. The deafening silence was sacred. My heart was content knowing whose arms my child was in while still wrestling with a hole I knew would never be filled by anything or anyone else.

Tears tumbled again on a not-so-ordinary Sunday. It was Mother's Day, just eleven short days after I'd placed my daughter in the arms of her adoptive mom.

As the church pastor asked moms to stand, I deliberated. Should I dare stand? Tears of both heartache and joy flowed from a full heart that had faced a heart-wrenching loss. Tangled emotions spilled out. I knew what I had to do.

On that first Mother's Day after I'd made an adoption plan for my daughter as an unwed teenage girl, I couldn't deny that I was now a mom. Hesitantly rising to my feet, overwhelmed by emotion, I stood. I stood, proud of my daughter, proud of myself, but mostly, humbled and in awe of the place the Lord had so profoundly led us. He had met us every step of the way. He stood with me. He was with my daughter. He had seen us and was with us both. As He always will be.

Traci Robinson

Traci relishes the never-ending journey of discovering the Father's redemptive heart as He leads her as His daughter, as a mama, and as a writer. One of her favorite parts about walking with Jesus is the way He surprises her with way better plans than hers throughout the many seasons of life. He's always up to something good. She loves writing about all the times He's brought beauty from ashes in her life. She studied at Rocky Mountain Bible Institute, Colorado Christian University and earned a master's degree in social work from the University of Denver. Traci loves living in the beauty of Colorado, married to her soulmate, who happens to be her eight-grade boyfriend. They keep busy with their sometimes chaotic, but always beautiful, blended family of eight. You can learn more about Traci at AmberForAshes.com.

🌐 www.AmberForAshes.com

In the Middle of Nowhere
Karen Crowfoot

I remember packing my suitcase. Jeans, check. T-shirts, check. Dress and high heels for wedding, check. The next day my parents and I were going on a road trip traveling east from Colorado to Iowa to attend a family wedding. Having had my license for just 4 months, I was a proud, but inexperienced driver. I asked my dad if I could drive the first leg of our journey. I have no recollection of anything else which occurred that fateful day.

We never made it to the wedding. The highway was two-lane and in disrepair with no shoulders. It had been 2 hours and I was getting tired of driving. I tried to pass a car and another was coming toward us in the passing lane. I quickly returned to our lane. The right tires of our compact car went off the road. Then I over-corrected and we rolled, flying over the barbed wire fence and landing in a barren field in eastern Colorado.

It was a horrific accident; a wonder anyone survived. Our car had landed on its roof, flattening the driver's side. My parents were in shock, but escaped, sustaining minor injuries. I remained in the car, hanging up-side-down by the seat belt shoulder strap. The position of my neck squeezed my airway and my face had turned blue from lack of oxygen.

Simultaneously, in the sovereignty of God, a teenager from St. Louis who was my age was driving the same model car, traveling west on the same highway with his parents. Both of us were novice drivers who followed the speed limit. He arrived at the scene of our accident at just the right time. Had either of us been speeding, it is very likely we would have missed each other. Several cars and a semi had stopped on the side of the road by our overturned car. He slowed down and convinced his dad to stop and help. Going through the shattered glass of the back window, the father and son found me suspended by the seat belt. In God's perfect timing and grace, I miraculously gasped for air as they stabilized my neck and carefully lowered me to the ground!

When the paramedics finally arrived, my rescuer was adamant as he gave specific instructions not to move my neck more than necessary while they transferred me from the car to the ambulance.

My spinal cord had been bruised during the roll-over, resulting from a dislocation and fracture of my cervical vertebrae. I was left with permanent, partial paralysis from the neck down. Surely, I would have died within minutes or my spinal cord been severed causing complete paralysis if my good Samaritan and his son had not stopped and exercised such timely care. My divinely-appointed rescuer just happened to be a neurologist, who was in the right place at the right time, in a field, in the middle of nowhere.

Karen Crowfoot

Karen grew up in a military family so has had the opportunity to live in many different places and get to know people from all walks of life. She made a commitment to follow Christ at an early age. Karen began swimming competitively at the age of ten and learned perseverance and fortitude during the next six years. During that time, she became a high school All-American by swimming the last leg of the medley relay setting a Colorado high school state record.

Her Christian faith and perseverance has carried her through many trials including a devastating auto accident when she was sixteen resulting in a spinal cord injury and chronic pain. After her accident, she obtained a degree in Speech Pathology and has worked in the field for thirty-two years treating speech, language, swallowing, and cognitive disorders. She has great empathy for her patients as she understands the implications of a life-changing event. She can still be found enjoying the pool and swims several days a week. Karen has been married to her husband, Rick, for twenty-five years. Among her greatest privileges has been being mom to two young adults, an outstanding daughter and son.

Hilarious Healing
B D Johnson

It was pressing toward mid-autumn. Weather patterns seemed to change more often in Colorado than the clock changed hours. I got the call I did not want. Mom died. I had talked to her more often recently, but needed to find time for a visit. My brothers and I quickly settled on a date to have a memorial service, and a time to be together to share, laugh and catch up on each other's lives. I hurriedly finished some work so I could get paid before I headed to northern Illinois.

Three days before the event, the temperature here was in the low seventies. I packed my small pickup with my guitar and snacks and clothes for all seasons, then debated in my mind what time to leave. I loved driving long distances and even going alone, sometimes driving through the night. But I was tired and took a nap.

At 2:30 a.m. I awoke, later than I wanted. The trip could take sixteen hours in good weather, and I desired to be there for supper. When I stepped outside it was very warm. I took off my coat, loaded myself in the truck, and headed to the highway. A few hours later I took a bathroom break, and it still felt like summer.

About half an hour after I started driving again, a light snow was falling. It did not take long before I was driving into a blinding blizzard covering the lines on the road. The only thing visible was an occasional reflector off to the right, so I wouldn't drive into the ditch. My eyes became very tired, so I looked for an exit sign. I thought about resting until there was at least a shred of daylight. But the ramp was closed for construction. I parked by the side of the road for a few minutes and prayed, "God, You need to be my eyes, and I know Your angels are with me guiding and keeping me safe. I need You to take me through this storm." I pulled back on the interstate, but did not dare drive fast. I was watching in the rear-view mirror for any lights that might be approaching, but no one else was on the road. It was the snow, angels around my pickup. God's presence, and me. Then without any sound or sign that anything was near, a semi-truck appeared in the left lane ahead of my truck, then moved into my lane. My tires fell right into line with the inside tires of his duals. It picked up speed until we were moving way faster, it seemed, than we should in those conditions. I asked God if I should be driving this fast. Yet I was prompted by Holy Spirit, that I should stay the same distance from the back of the semi as I was when it moved in front of me.

We proceeded at that speed for well more than an hour, and the entire time there were no other tracks in the snow, and no lights from other vehicles. We drove in Heaven's deep silence until daylight began to break. Like we drove out of a cave, we were suddenly passing other trucks and vehicles, close to one every quarter mile. No one else was driving our speed or coming up behind us. As soon as there was enough daylight to see where I was and where I needed to be, we passed a truck that shot a light spray across my windshield. I swished the wipers once. The truck leading me was nowhere in sight.

I pulled off at one of the next exits and checked the mileage. I had logged close to three hundred and fifty miles in barely over four and a half hours. The rest of the journey was mostly through rain showers, but was fairly easy. I arrived at my destination at about the fourteen-hour mark.

We brothers had a great time together. Our conversations and humor made that time, the memorial service, and dealing with mom's things, much easier and less sad. The four of us had always found laughter. If something wasn't funny one of us would make a pun or turn it in a way that had us all in stitches. I missed that living so far away. The leaving part was hard to endure.

I headed back to Colorado with sadness in my heart and tears occasionally flowing from my eyes. The morning was dark with heavy fog just like I was. I dropped to a depth in my soul I had not known since dad died nine years earlier.

I attempted to sing through the grief, including singing prayers. The weather and I both began to clear some by late morning.

At least the afternoon drive was easier on my mind as I kept to back roads and slowed through small towns, taking in better scenery than along the four-lane highway. I even stopped for most of an hour at one of my favorite burger joints. It was snowing when I made it home but I was able to park in a sheltered spot so I wouldn't have to unload until morning. I did not take into account how my body was feeling, and crashed for the night.

When I awoke the next morning, I tried to stand like I normally could. But it felt like I was one huge cramp from my hips to my feet. I forced myself to walk, thinking I just needed to move around and gain some flexibility in my legs and all would be back the way it should be. My right leg responded, but my left side was refusing to cooperate with my self-therapy. The next day I went to a chiropractic appointment for non-self-therapy. I found I had sciatic nerve pain from my left lower back, down my leg to the top of my foot. I'm sure the stress and emotional pain of losing mom along with driving two thousand miles took its toll on every part of my being - mind, soul, and body. I had eaten so many things not good for me in the past few weeks as well as getting almost no exercise, and my body was not reacting well.

It took a couple of months before the pain subsided, but the discomfort and cramping did not go away. My left ankle still did not want to flex the way God had created it. I had been a runner most of my life, and having a good heel strike with my right foot and a flat-footed plod with my left was not fun. Then God began to show me a new foot position and a new way to strike the ground. With that I could sprint easily but would start to hurt after a mile or so...and the cramps still came.

I settled for being like that for too long. Several years later, a couple was hosting a series of meetings, teaching such great confidence in God that nothing the devil threw at them ever bothered them. I was compelled to attend. On Saturday morning they presented a number of scenarios that might make people anxious or stressed or angry or fearful, then prompted us to laugh at those things that confront us. We laughed at pain and sickness, or financial problems and loss, or worries or lack of jobs or life woes.

Several people including myself got to laughing hard and couldn't stop. When pauses in teaching came, we found that other people were laughing at us laughing. It was the Holy Spirit lightness that releases after living in heaviness and through tough times. I remembered a record that my dad had picked up.

It was called "It's In the Book"* preached by Johnny Standley. People laughed at funny lines about Little Bo Peep losing her sheep. There was one guy laughing that perfectly illustrates uncontrollable laughter. When I was a child, I would laugh hard at all kinds of things. I was created, even as an adult, to create acts of humor for those around me. I performed skit acting and stand-up comedy. But that waned for many years of my life.

Lunch break came. I went outside intending to hobble to a fast-food place. But my ankle and foot felt different. I took off running...easy at first, then faster. I burst into a strong sprint and kept it for a quarter mile. It felt so good I did it again... and again. God had healed everything down my left side...by laughing.

The Bible has no verse that specifically says "laugh and be healed", but I've heard laughing is really good medicine. There are many verses referring to merriment and cheerfulness and taking delight in God and His goodness.

I recently perused the aspects of Advent.

That we can live in great hope.

Anything that seems hard for us doesn't have to last forever.

That God's incomprehensible peace is a catalyst for healing our hearts and bodies.

That seasons of joy in our lives have the power to help us stay healthy in mind and body.

That we are created to be love as God's image is love. For He loves to give His good gifts and to heal.

We can live in those truths for our lives and our bodies. And also allow them to tumble out to those around us.

Many times others can experience miracles just by the word of our testimony.

Live expectantly and thank God for all His goodness.

And keep laughing through it all.

* You can look it up - "It's In the Book" Johnny Standley 1952 Capitol 2249

B D Johnson

B D Johnson grew up in home, church and social settings where active imagination was encouraged. He made up stories that made himself and others either laugh or cry, and wrote much of what was floating through his mind. As a teen he and his brother began performing short comedic skits for events. That led him to co-write plays and music that would be performed at larger events, and eventually to some stand-up comedy. He is also published in a couple of anthologies.

He got busy with other ways of helping people, mostly in prayer for personal challenges and healing, and wrote very little for many years. Later in life he was invited to produce small group worship music that got him mostly writing lyrics. He began to have vivid dreams in the night through which God restored the spark of imagination by having him write short inspirational declarations as well as music and even comedy routines. Then several dreams turned into longer stories and he was again hooked on writing and performing.

Holy Spirit is now prompting him to share many God encounters, miracles, and stories by publishing them for a greater audience, inspiring healing and bringing light and hope in story form to many who have lived through life's challenges.

✉ mrbryan62@gmail.com

My Love Story: Spirit, Soul and Body
Rebekah Lind

When I finally met my husband, there was a lot God had done in my life that had prepared me to see him and recognize he was the man I could build a life with. Although I had a dream, a list, a time frame, a plan; it didn't happen that way. I had given God permission to guide my life, and He met me there and exceeded my expectations, fulfilled my list, shifted my time frame for my best interest, and superseded my plan with His, which was much better. Let me share with you how God met me with the answers I needed to step into a lifelong relationship with the best man for me.

When I met my husband for the first time, I had just turned thirty-one. I'd been in a couple of serious relationships that seemed headed toward marriage but ended in heartbreak, even though I knew that was the best decision. I tried to continue to hold on to hope because I was delighting myself in the Lord, He would fulfill the desires of my heart (Psalm 37:4), which included a husband and children. After my previous break up, I had designed an engagement band for myself as a way of cultivating hope, and I began keeping a journal with letters to my future husband and praying for him. I was participating in a class at my church called Single Life Workshop, in an effort to grow in my interactions with men, to combat the fear there was something wrong with me and that's why no one was pursuing me and I was still single. I was maintaining hope by attempting to be proactive in meeting men and preparing myself for healthy relationship within a marriage.

A friend of mine invited me to a Ceroc dance lesson she and her brother were teaching, but I came late because I'd been at a hip hop dance class that overlapped with the start time of the Ceroc class. I danced with several men that night, including my future husband. He made some false assumptions about his observations of me and one of his roommates asked me out that night. As we continued to run into each other in common activities—home group, a climbing group, recreational dance classes—God turned our hearts toward each other and opened our eyes to see something we may not have previously seen. He asked me out one evening at home group and although I was not attracted to him, I said I'd go out because I was impressed he had the courage to ask. I knew from my observation he was a good guy and I had been so frustrated with what seemed to me to be a lack of courage or confidence in men to ask a lady out. This decision had been influenced by what I'd been learning in the Single Life Workshop (SLW) as well.

We went out on a few dates and I was enjoying the male attention and getting to know him, but wasn't ready to commit to a relationship like he was. I tried to communicate this; however, he didn't hear what I was trying to say. He thought I was asking him to leave me alone. I felt disappointed when he quit pursuing me so I asked to have another conversation and we realized our communication had fallen down. Once we figured that out, we continued to spend time together. Because he was such a romantic and was doing a good job of trying to woo me, I really wanted to like him more than I did. I put a lot of pressure on myself to figure out whether he was "the one" quickly and I was determined not to settle for anything less than what I'd asked God for in a husband. People had questioned my convictions wondering whether I was being too picky and so I went back to that scripture in Psalms 37:4 and talked to the Lord about it. I felt Him remind me that He loved the desires of my heart, in fact He'd placed them there and He was big enough to meet them. He wasn't asking me to settle for anything less than His best, which included all of my desires and more.

After about two and a half months of getting to know him, there were four things that still bothered me and made me feel hesitant about entering into a serious relationship with him. One, his laugh really annoyed me. It felt loud and obnoxious and embarrassing to me. Two, he felt to me like he was shorter than I was, and I had always wanted a man who could wrap his arms around me and envelope me. Three, he was so intense and loud and always seemed to be joking around, that I didn't know if I could handle that level of intensity continually day in and day out, wondering if he could ever have a serious, meaningful conversation. And four, I still wasn't super attracted to him physically. Although most of these things seemed petty to me and I felt bad not being able to just ignore them. I felt like I needed to pay attention in order to be true to myself. So, I had a conversation with him and told him I wasn't ready to move into a more committed relationship with him and didn't want to lead him on since I was undecided and he clearly wasn't. But I did ask him if we could try to just be friends. Hoping it would take the pressure off of trying to decide if I wanted to spend the rest of my life with him, and just get to know each other without the dating piece clouding my judgement. We agreed to take the pressure off of where the relationship was heading in order to be more present in the now. I secretly hoped this would give him a chance to prove himself and be in my life long term—and try to start again by just being friends. This conversation was actually one of the best conversations I'd had with him because I felt the pressure release and we continued to enjoy chatting for quite a while after the initial communication.

That conversation was the beginning of dispelling my fears of his over intensity and my wondering whether we could connect emotionally and seriously about things that mattered.

Around the same time, I had this conversation with him, we'd done a session at SLW about the importance of blessing our spirit man and nurturing that part of who we are. We had all blessed each other's spirits within our small group. Although I enjoyed learning about this aspect of who we are, when my small group blessed my spirit, I don't remember it being an impacting or significant encounter. However, within a week or ten days there was a clear shift in my feelings and perspective towards Jesse, my future husband.

One Saturday night we both attended an open dance night where there was a short lesson at the beginning and then an extended time of dancing with various partners and practicing the dance moves we'd learned. The venue was new but we'd been attending the class for several months as we'd been getting to know each other. I think that evening was the first time we'd seen each other since I'd had my spirit blessed. I'm convinced that something happened in my spirit after I was blessed that allowed me to see things through the eyes of the Spirit of God. At one point during the evening, I was dancing with someone else and I heard Jesse's laughter across the room and it dawned on me it felt endearing instead of irritating. That got my attention! Later in the evening I was dancing with him and I realized for the first time he was a couple of inches taller than I was. I couldn't believe I was only now seeing it, several months after we'd been spending time together. I began to feel a shift in my heart towards him that night as I reflected on the things that had kept me from wanting to enter a serious relationship with him. None of these things seemed to be an issue any longer. As I spent time with the Lord, I realized He had shifted my perspective and ability to see things as they truly were instead of how I had seen them. I traced it back to a shift in my spirit man. Now I was able to see through the eyes of my spirit as well as my physical eyes and together they shifted my perspective. I had been opened in a new way to hearing and seeing situations and people from God's perspective because a part of me I hadn't been as in tune with was now awakened.

With those hesitations out of the way, I was becoming more eager to develop relationship with Jesse. I was beginning to feel attracted to him physically, although I gave myself time before sharing that with him. I wanted to confirm clearly with the Lord that He was leading me to pursue and allow myself to be pursued by Jesse. But eventually the confirmation was clear and I couldn't hold back anymore from sharing my discoveries with Jesse. This revelation ended up leading us into a relationship, engagement, and marriage eight months later. While I had done my due diligence—getting to know the man Jesse was—and held onto the hope of Psalm 37:4, the Lord had met me in a way I never could have anticipated, He helped me grow personally in my spiritual walk with Him through the experience. He proved His word to be true in my life, upheld my conviction to hold on to hope that all I wanted could be a reality, and led me every step of the way into one of the most important decisions one can ever make. God created marriage and had laid it on my heart to desire it. He met me where I was, drew me closer to Him as my spirit was awakened to Him in the process, and used that experience to ultimately fulfill one of the biggest dreams in my heart. This was also the beginning of learning how to engage my spirit man with my soul and body in living life, cultivating my marriage and raising my children. Little did I know that one 'small' encounter, the significance of which I didn't even understand at the time, would lead to a more fulfilled and deeper relationship with the Lord throughout my life, as opposed to just a moment where He met me when I was so desperately searching for one answer. He came and answered but took it so many steps above and beyond and is still working to this day, teaching me about spirit, soul and body unity in my life.

Rebekah Lind

Rebekah Lind was born in the USA and has also lived in Johannesburg, South Africa and Melbourne, Australia. She loves to travel and experience culture, whether it's language, art, customs, or sports that shape people. She holds an English Education degree and taught middle school and high school for five years before changing careers and getting back into her first love, dance. She has a heart for regional dance ministry and to see unity among dance movements across the church of Jesus Christ. This book represents the fulfillment of two life-long dreams: to write books and to be a mother. She enjoys reading, creating mixed media artwork, playing with and teaching her boys, and spending time with family and friends.

Connect with Rebekah and stay encouraged on your journey of parenting by visiting her website spiritledcreative.space

⊕ spiritledcreative.space

A Miracle in Alaska During the Pandemic

Constance Kay Thompson

Miracles do happen. God has intervened in my life many times over the past eighty-four years and has always pointed me in a better direction.

But this time it was different!

"I can't breathe! I can't breathe!" was what my husband would hear me say over and over for all of May and June 2020 right during the middle of the pandemic.

The ER was my only go to destination for those two months. So much so, the ER staff would greet me with, "You Again!" They just loved me so much that finally, on several different occasions they just decided to just keep me in the hospital. During COVID, it was very lonely and scary. Big masks were worn by all the staff. Some were wearing all the head-to-toe COVID gear. The staff and all the doctors were kind to me and took very good care of me which did give me some comfort.

You see, I had a serious, and I guess quite complicated heart problem, for which my cardiologist, Dr. Suneet Pirohit, worked patiently to find a solution. He just would not give up. He had several cardiologists assisting him from time to time to help find the right solution for my heart problem. Several surgeons stopped by my room too, which gave me comfort. After several days had gone by, one of the cardiologists started bringing me a donut each morning before he started his rounds.

After I had been in and out of the hospital for several weeks during those two months, the hospital doctor came to my room and told me many specialists had concluded they had done everything possible for me. She made it clear, I was not going to survive this heart problem. The hospital staff prepared me as best they could, it was only a matter of time that my weakened heart would give out.

I was facing certain death.

It was during COVID. My husband and family could not be with me. I felt so alone.

I would challenge myself to walk the halls with the little energy I had left. My favorite destination was the place I could gaze out on to the beautiful, calming, peaceful gardens. Only a very few people were ever in those gardens. I would go back to my room and ask the nurses, "Why can't I go out there? Maybe even have my husband meet me there. We would be outside and promise to practice social distancing."

They all said, "Oh, no. It's COVID and that is against all the hospital rules."

That night, I believe God intervened!

The next morning, Brett, a very kind nurse came into my room and said, "Call your husband and tell him to meet you in twenty minutes in the Peace Garden! Now, come with me!"

That was the happiest time during those two lonely months. How wonderful! We held each other so close it seemed like we became one.

Back in the hospital the palliative care team were preparing me for the conference call I needed to make with my family. They counseled me about what I needed to say. A family teleconference was arranged! My son and daughter-in-law, their two adult children in California, my son and daughter-in-law in Anchorage, and my husband were now ready to listen to this surreal conversation. I guess I must have told them what I was supposed to, funeral-no funeral, cremation- burial, burial location, obituary-no obituary, music, etc. etc.

Now if you think that was hard for me to do, imagine what it must have felt like for my family who dearly loves me to hear my voice telling them my end of life wishes.

"Is this for real?" I kept asking myself. Since I only had myself to talk to, I never got an answer.

A couple days later, the hospital doctor came to my room and said, "You can go home tomorrow. Go home and make yourself comfortable and call hospice!"

"WHAT? Call hospice! Really?"

That was the moment it really sunk in. I was going to die.

So, how did I feel? It took me awhile to realize my family would soon have to learn how to live without me.

"No, I can't let this happen," I kept saying to myself over and over; praying and praying.

With God's help, I was able to keep calm, but I remember having a strong fighting spirit inside me. I found myself asking, "How would my husband get along without me? Then my two sons, I know they would miss me terribly. And what about all of my six grandchildren, especially my youngest granddaughter. She is only thirteen; much too young to lose her grandmother."

The next day, I was sent home with discharge papers and a list of all the mortuaries in Anchorage.

I guess it is final. I really am going to die!

It feels wonderful being home and in the arms of my family. There was a strange tension because none of us talked about the inevitable.

Several days later, Dr. Pirohit called me, my husband, and my son back into his office. I knew Dr. Pirohit never gave up on me. Maybe that is why I felt a calmness through this whole thing. He also had a cardiovascular surgeon in the room with us, Dr. Matt Maxwell.

Dr. Pirohit sat down in front of me. "Connie, you are going downhill. You are not going to make it. However, there is one last thing we can try for you. That is open heart surgery. We usually do not do surgery on someone as old as you, but Dr. Maxwell is willing to do this surgery."

Of course, then he told us of all the risks and said it was our choice.

He told us, I may not survive the open heart surgery; but for sure we all knew I did not have a chance if we did not try it. Within minutes, we all agreed.

"Yes, have Dr. Matt Maxwell perform open heart surgery."

Dr. Maxwell gave us his PERSONAL cell phone number and we communicated several times over the next three days. On the fourth day Dr. Matt Maxwell held my heart in his hands. Along with his surgical team and God's help, he performed a miracle that changed my life forever!

I will always be indebted to Dr. Matt Maxwell, and Dr. Pirohit. I have prayed for them every day since that miraculous surgery day, June 24, 2020, and will continue to do so. Next to my husband, they are the two most important men in my life. Not only did they save my life, they have not forgotten me, and have become close friends.

One year later, I have my life back, enjoying my family and friends. I am healthier now than I have been in more than twenty-five years and still continuing to get better every day. My family has a much more active eighty-five-year-old wife, mother, and grandmother.

Who of you would not say, "This was truly a miracle!"

Constance Kay Thompson

Constance Kay Thomas, better known as Connie, and her six siblings grew up a homestead in Eastern Montana in a house without electricity or indoor plumbing.

After being homeschooled for eight years, Connie attended a public high school which was fifty miles from her home. She received her bachelor's degree in Elementary Education after attending St. Olaf College and Montana State College.

Connie taught school in Montana for three years before marrying her husband and moving to Alaska. She taught in Fairbanks for three years while homesteading and earning her master's degree in Elementary Education.

After leaving Fairbanks, Connie worked in the Anchorage school district for ten years and then transferred to the Arctic Circle in Alaska where she taught Eskimo children in two different villages.

After six years in the Arctic, Connie and her husband took a teaching position on the equator in Surabaya, Indonesia at a private International School. After six years, She and her family returned to the United States and moved to Homer, Alaska, where Connie owned and operated her own private preschool and day care for the next twelve years.

Connie and her husband have three grown children and six grandchildren They are semi-retired and live in Anchorage, Alaska.

November 1977
Sharon Burrell

I really did not know who JESUS was, and certainly did not believe I could have a personal relationship with Him. My husband's grandmother, who I called "Grandma", had been telling about the Lord and encouraging me to read my Bible. This was a lot for someone who had only been in church twice, once for Easter and once for Christmas. Not only had I never read the Bible, I don't remember ever seeing one in our home. To hear Grandma talking about and to a God I could not see was different; although my heart longed for what she seemed to possess. She was more assured in what she did not see than I was in what I did see.

I tried to follow Grandma's instructions and read the Bible every day. I kept being led to Psalm 51 and Psalm 91, but I had no clarity or insight to what the psalmist was saying and how it applied to me or my family's lives.

My husband and I were married right out of high school at eighteen and nineteen years of age. Both coming from dysfunction and hurt but determined when we had children it would be different, and our children would not go through what we had endured. Little did we know that we would be blessed with two beautiful daughters exactly eleven months apart to the day after only twenty-one months of marriage. Each of us responded differently to this sudden increase in our family and change in circumstances.

Given the fact I was the eldest of eight and had assisted my mother with my siblings after school, as well as some evenings and weekends, I had more experience. My husband's experience was different. He and his brother, who was six years younger, were raised by a single mother.

Of course, I was off from work, and our growing family had to survive on one income. Something we had not planned for. We hadn't expected the strain it would cause on our relationship either.

Most of my days and nights were spent taking care of the children and home while my husband went to work to support our family. My husband certainly loved his daughters, however, to relieve the presser of it all, he would to hang out with his associates, go drinking, and take long rides alone. When he was home, he would engage with the girls; then he left to clean, work on his car, or go to visit his mother, brother and stepfather.

I felt abandoned, alone, and rejected. I had no girlfriends or family despite the fact I had relatives everywhere. I didn't have anyone to talk to about so many of things on my heart. I did have my cousin, however, was in a very abusive relationship herself. Considering what she was dealing with I thought it unfair to burden her with my issues. I could call Grandma anytime but because she had been saved all her life there were things, I just didn't believe she would understand and therefore I would not discuss them with her. But I knew I could ask her to pray about anything and she would.

Most of the conversations between me and my husband were about the children, which were usually cordial. If the subject of his behavior was brought up, he was quick to remind me he was grown and could do what he wanted. When I cried and became upset, he would tell me I was too sensitive and he wasn't stopping me from working if I wanted to, we would just have to agree on acceptable childcare. So, all the emotional support had vanished, there were no longer moments that we went out anywhere.

After three years I felt totally drained; alone, unsupported, and desperate. I loved my children dearly and had no regrets; however, I had not taken care of me. What had I done to get to this place and what could I do to be free again?

One night with a very heavy heart I called Grandma. I told her what was going on and asked her to pray. This time I asked her to pray that if there really was a God, He would not allow me to wake up in the morning. She inquired what would happen to my two daughters.

I responded, "My husband would take them to his mother, who always wanted girls."

She replied, "She struggles with her own two. Why would you do that?"

She then told me she would pray with me, but not what I asked. She proceeded to speak to God. After she prayed, she told me not to worry. I went to sleep keeping in mind what I wanted her to pray versus what she did pray right then. Then, I drifted off to sleep.

The next day I got up and completed my routine with my daughters until it was time for them to take their nap. At this time, I went and sat on the porch right outside their windows. I realized I was still here, and I did not feel the weight I had the night before! I sat and looked at the grass, the birds, the trees, and the sky. I continued to open and close my eyes as it looked as if someone had painted the world with fluorescent paint. As I started to cry uncontrollably, I heard clearly in my spirit "If I take care of the grass and trees that come up without any help from man; and the birds are cared for how much more won't I take care of you".

I got up and started in the house, running into my neighbor from the other side of the duplex. She asked what was wrong. I invited her to come and see. I began telling her what I was seeing, and asked if she could see it, too.

She hugged me and said, "the Lord has opened your eyes."

I ran in and immediately called Grandma who instructed me to call "700 Club" to pray the sinner's prayer. I followed her instructions. Afterwards I contacted, Billy Graham, Rex Humbard, and Oral Roberts and ordered their bible studies and ordered a KJV Bible from Rex Humbard. I began to feeding and filling my spirit man as I did my physical man daily

Then I called my mother and told her I forgave her for everything and ask for her forgiveness of me if I had done anything to her.

From there I began my journey with a Loving Father. I had a NEW HEART A NEW MIND and HE created a desire to fill them with HIS WORD and Understanding. I was being EQUIPPED.

Sharon Burrell

Sharon Burrell is the President and CEO of KINGDOM Service Training & Consulting. She is a wife and mother of seven for the past forty-six years, and believes dreams can become reality. She also believes knowledge alone is not power, but knowledge combined with precise action is true power.

Through a variety of training programs Mrs. Burrell has developed a mission to provide women and minorities the counseling, training, and technical assistance necessary to start a new business, successfully operate or expand a existing business, or develop and make career changes.

Being a business owner for the past thirty years, while raising a family and completing a dual Ph.D., ABD program, Mrs. Burrell has a sensitivity, compassion, and awareness of the power of effective communication. Words can bring people together and fuel fulfillment of dreams. Sharon enjoys helping anyone she can, however, she holds a special passion for individuals and their families with autism and mental health diagnosis.

Co-Parenting with God

Tracy Fagan

Train up a child in the way he should go,
And when he is old he will not depart from it.
Proverbs 22:6 NKJV

I am a proud mom of an "almost-grown" daughter. I say that because she is under the age of twenty-five, so the prefrontal cortex of her brain isn't fully developed yet; or maybe it's just a mom's desire to hang on a little longer. Either way, she is doing a great job of transitioning from being a dependent teen to becoming an independent young adult. She is moving ahead in her career, living on her own, and successfully paying her own bills. She has even given me two grand-kittens.

The one area of her life that isn't looking like MY design is her relationship with God. When I brought my concern to God's attention, He told me to let go of my plans and trust Him. He then reminded me of the first time my daughter was introduced to Jesus…which was not my plan either.

Back when I was a little girl, our family went to church every Sunday and my sister and I attended a Catholic elementary school. I knew the name Jesus and had a belief in God. One thing that always irked me was having to get to service early on Christmas and Easter to make sure we got a seat. As a little girl, I vowed if I ever decided to not attend church regularly, then I wouldn't go on Christmas or Easter either, taking the seats of the faithful ones.

As I started the journey of my life as an independent young adult, I stopped going to church on Sundays. Staying true to my word, I also stopped going on Christmas and Easter. Soon, I found myself with no connection to God.

I got busy with life; started my career, got married, and had a child. Then came the December when God started to get my attention.

It was entertaining to watch my eighteen-month-old daughter's anticipation about Santa's pending arrival. She would bubble over with excitement talking about the presents he might bring. There was joy in decorating her first gingerbread house.

Our nighttime routine helped to fuel the holiday excitement by reading books about Santa, presents, and snowmen. One night, when reading about snowmen coming to life, I felt something was missing.

Pondering my childhood Christmas memories, the thing that was missing became evident; Baby Jesus. My little girl didn't even know the name Jesus. Let alone that Christmas was the celebration of His birth.

There was no spiritual element in our home. I felt awkward asking my husband about buying our daughter a book about baby Jesus. We had been living without Jesus for many years, so why was it so important to have Him now?

A couple days after the revelation of the lack of Jesus in our Christmas traditions, I received a phone call from my mom.

"Good morning, Tracy. How are you doing today?"

"Hey, Mom. I'm good. Your granddaughter and I made a gingerbread house the other night, and she is getting excited for Santa to come."

"That sounds like fun. I am excited you guys are getting in the Christmas spirit. I know a big part of your routine is reading books. Do you have any Christmas books about the story of the nativity?" she asked hesitantly.

"Um, no. We don't," I said as conviction poked my heart.

"I don't want to overstep my bounds, but if you're ok with it, Dad and I would love to give you a book about Baby Jesus."

Tears began to well up in my eyes. "Yes, please. I was just thinking that my baby girl doesn't know the real meaning of the season."

"Ok. I'll pick one up and bring it over."

A few days later, my mom came by with a beautiful, yet simple book that told the story of Jesus' birth. We added it into our reading routine and God gave me the opportunity to introduce His baby girl to our Lord and Savior, Jesus Christ.

God met me that Christmas and gave both me and my daughter just what we needed to put the season in correct perspective. The first step in a long journey into a deeper relationship with Him.

In my recent conversation with God about my daughter's current relationship with Jesus, I tried giving Him ideas and pointers on how to win her over. He reminded me His relationship with each one of us is different, and not to judge what I see, because I can only see part of the picture. He also reminded me of the promise in His word; if we train up a child in the way they should go, when they grow old, they will not depart from it.

As parents, we are called to teach our children and help them grow physically, mentally, emotionally, and spiritually. The Christmas book about baby Jesus was God's idea, plan, and set-up to introduce Jesus to my daughter to begin her spiritual journey. I love how God met me back then to parent my daughter as a toddler, only to meet me again fifteen years later to offer more guidance. He reminded me she is still His daughter first; and He has the relationship between the two of them under control.

Tracy Fagan

Tracy Fagan is a fireball. She has experienced the transformational power of Jesus and loves to share her story through books, speaking, and teaching.

She is the founder of *Kingdom Publishing*, a Christ-centered book publisher. She uses over twenty-four years of marketing experience, creativity, and encouragement to help others fulfill their God-given assignments and bring their ideas and businesses to life.

She loves her native state of Colorado as well as experiencing different cultures through travel. You can find her hiking, skiing, working out, or swing dancing; but many times you will hear her laugh resonating before you see her. She is a proud mother to a beautiful "almost-adult" daughter.

🌐 www.TracyFagan.com
🌐 www.Kingdom-Publishing.com
📘 @Kingdom.Publish
📷 @Kingdom.Publish

How God Met Me in the Depth of My Fear
Michael Blaes

God meets us in some of the most exciting places. For me, it was outside of a hospital on a Saturday night. My wife, Teresa was having surgery on her knee the next day; and I was terrified. Teresa has a history of bad reactions to anesthesia. As we waited in her hospital room before her surgery, Teresa used our laptop to finish a poem. I sat there and watched her write, and it was like Satan himself was sitting on her shoulder, chuckling as he watched her. I could almost hear him say, "This is the last poem you will ever see her write." Then I saw a picture in my head of sitting in a waiting room by myself and having a doctor come in and tell me she died on the table.

I set out to take a walk and clear my mind. I put on Casting Crowns' "Praise you in the Storm." As I continued around the hospital, I could hear the Lord say, "My grace is sufficient for you; I will never leave you nor forsake you." It was like His love was washing over me; but I was so worried I could not take it in.

They were supposed to take Teresa to surgery at 7 a.m. the next day. But it kept getting delayed. Finally, the orderly showed up at about 1 p.m. We walked down to the operating room, and they started to prep her for the surgery. The anesthesiologist showed up a few minutes later and asked the preliminary questions. When Teresa admitted she had problems with anesthesia in the past, his tone changed. He walked away, came back a few minutes later, and told us he was postponing the surgery so they could do some tests and make sure he had an entire team available.

I breathed a sigh of relief. They took Teresa back to her room, and I walked down to the cafeteria to get something to eat. I ran into the anesthesiologist and told him how much I appreciated what he had done and for taking such great care of my wife.

I'll never forget what he told me. "I know how my medicines work, but I don't know what they will do inside your wife; that's why it is so important to delay the surgery." While he was talking, it was like I could hear the Holy Spirit saying, "Son, it's going to be okay, I've got this."

That evening, I received a phone call from our pastor. He asked me to confirm the rescheduled time of the surgery, and he told me he was going to send our friend Linda to be there with me. That was another answer to prayer. I wouldn't have to be alone in the waiting room. I was able to find a little peace.

The next day dawned. Teresa and I spent the morning praying and preparing for the surgery. Around 9:30 in the morning, the orderly came to get Teresa and took us to the operating room again. It was full speed ahead in the prep area. They started an IV and got her ready to go. A few minutes later, the same anesthesiologist came in, checked everything, and okayed Teresa for the surgery. He prayed with us, and a few minutes later, they rolled her into the operating room, and I was led to the waiting room. My friend Linda was there. She offered to take me to lunch because we expected Teresa to be in surgery for a couple of hours. I left my number with the waiting room monitor, and we went.

We ended up going to a Mexican restaurant across the street. It was very crowded and noisy. We ordered our food. By the time we got our order, my cell phone had rung. It was the waiting room monitor. Because of the noise level in the restaurant, I could not hear the caller. We packed up our food and headed back to the hospital. By the time we got back to the waiting room, I had missed getting the report from the doctor. It was upsetting because I had no idea how Teresa was doing. Finally, the monitor went to the recovery area to check on her for me. The monitor returned and told me that Teresa was out of surgery and getting ready to be moved to recovery.

She was in stable condition. I sat there a little longer praising God, but still nervous.

Finally, I couldn't stand it any longer, and approached the waiting room monitor again to check on her. She smiled, and told me Teresa was fully awake and was getting ready to go back to her room. I started to head back to my seat, and then I saw my beautiful wife as they rolled her by. I walked back to the room with her and rejoiced. They told me later that Teresa came out from under anesthesia in under fifteen minutes. I could feel the peace of the Lord wash over me.

That night, I took another stroll around the hospital. I had my Walkman playing, and once again, "Praise You in the Storm" start playing. I felt my spirit soar as the words reminded me to lift my head because God is God; not matter where I am. And that God holds my hand, even when my heart is torn. That is why I praise Him even through life's storms. I heard the voice of the Lord just as I did before. "My grace is sufficient for you. I will never leave you nor forsake you." This time I kept saying, "Yes Lord!" over and over again.

God met me in the depths of my fear; in the middle of my storm. I know beyond a shadow of a doubt, He will always be with me. He will never leave me nor forsake me. Just give Him a chance; I know He will do the same for you.

Michael Blaes

Michael is an author, poet, speaker, and entrepreneur. Together, with his wife Teresa, He founded Kadosh Media, a podcast production company whose purpose is to give the Remnant of God's People a voice. They live in Alamogordo, New Mexico with their special needs daughter Mandy and their three cats, Monkey, Rascal, and Abby.

One Day Does Matter
Daniel Fariss

No matter how you meet Jesus, the impact is the same. The moment were my mind heart and soul were in the correct place tends to get a lot of attention. However, my sister in-law accepted Jesus Christ as her Savior at a young age with a simple prayer and not a lot of baggage or drama, and her story has the same beautiful end; eternity with God. Please, if you get anything from this, collect the thought, Jesus came to meet your need and died for your sin.

My story:

I never stood out in school. I got along with a lot of people, was terrible in class (sorry to all my teachers), didn't excel at sports or activities other that drinking and socializing. I was blessed because without my knowledge, my mother and a friend's mother, who also was a pastor, prayed for me a lot. Right after I graduated high school, I was presented with a scenario that led me in to the US Army.

I went to basic training with excitement and high hopes. The agreement was simple. They feed and house me, and I follow directions. Basic training, believe it or not, was fun and adventurous for me. I truly enjoyed the challenge. The problems started at my first post in Germany. I was so excited to travel and see the world. Due to the fact I was the only soldier from the Western USA I had twenty-one days of leave when everyone else had only twenty.

Please understand the trials I am about to tell here is God preparing me to meet Jesus.

One day does matter; never forget that. That one day required the orders to be put together by hand, and the person who did that task mistakenly misspelled my last name by one letter. Instead of Fariss they put Farris. When I checked in to Germany, no one caught this so I appeared as an unknown soldier; and I was reported as AWOL. Three months of regular military service went by before I was detained.

They started with charging me with writing bad checks. From there, it quickly went from bad to worse. I didn't have a relationship with God, but I started a journey of asking why and how all this could happen.

The next year and a half were an absolute nightmare. I was on extra duty, food restrictions, and no pay. And if that wasn't enough, I had to support other units in the field. Because of my schedule I was isolated and never had time to really find out what happened. When my time in the army ended, I had become bitter and depressed.

Despite the trials, God protected my name. Around the time the dishonorable discharge was being processed, information came forward that cleared up the situation. From this experience, I became very independent. I trusted no one. I adopted the policy, if I personally couldn't make work, I did not need it.

Back Home:

After my discharge from the military, I found myself very isolated. For the first time since I was thirteen years old, I could not find a job. I was living in my parents' home (back in the 1990s that was bad). Most of my friends had moved on in life. Feeling I had gained nothing from the Army, no college, and a high school push out, I was alone.

I finally got a job and moved in with a friend I reconnected with. My driver's license had been suspended soon after I went into the military. However, I was allowed to ride a motorcycle to work. It can be treacherous in Colorado in the winter.

Because of the isolation, and having to do everything myself in the Army, I was in the habit of not sharing or asking for help. In February 1993, I started to ask God, "Why?" I was drinking, alone, and saw no future.

The Holy Spirit answered my question by putting it on my heart to go visit churches. I found it easy to be invisible in the church I grew up in, and I wanted to find this elusive God thing.

Having no clue about different denominations, and with my motorcycle as my only mode of transportation in the Colorado winter, I started close to home and worked my way out. It felt like I visited every church in the Denver area.

The reaction from those who attended these different churches fell into two categories: either they felt they knew me and my past, and stayed clear, treating me like a leper or, not knowing me, they stayed clear, not inviting me in, or reaching out.

The Moment God Showed Up.

I was at a breaking point. Discouraged; feeling as though God had marked me as "not acceptable."

The day before St. Patrick's Day of 1993, being drunk and dismayed, I looked toward the sky. I simply said, "God, if You do not want me then I will make the best of this life on my own."

Feeling a nudge to look one last time for a church, I came across a St. Patrick's Day get together at a The Rocky Mountain Church for Singles. That night, there was some snow on the ground and it was a little over 30 degrees. As I showed up on my motorcycle, I notice there was one other bike in the parking lot. It caught my attention enough to encourage me go in. Thank you, Jesus!

I was not specifically looking for the rider of the other bike; however, I was having no luck in trying to strike a conversation. Inevitably the only person who would talk with me was Paul, they guy who rode the other bike. He was a genuine individual. He shared about God and how Christ had saved him from a life of drugs and depravity. I could relate, because that's where I was. He invited me to a home church for Sunday, and from that moment I was feeling a nurturing path to God.

I went to the home church with Paul several times and met with him one on one as well. They shared the gospel and really encouraged me. It was a true blessing.

Jesus took it all away?

I had decided that I, yes, I, would get my life together. I figured I would do this in steps. Quit drinking then smoking excreta. I was so excited I went to Paul's apartment to tell him. He was gone. Moved out; and I had no contact with the home church. I quickly found myself down and alone again. I decided I was going to find Jesus on my own. I already had a plan, I just needed to follow it. I slowed the drinking, cut the smoking down, and found a good church.

Even though I was making progress and the world saw improvement, since I was doing it all in my own strength, I was empty. On March 26, 1993, I was driving a large, fully loaded truck on an incredibly busy road. My plan was to smoke one cigarette every hour on the hour, and then cut back. This was my way of preparing myself to be acceptable to Jesus.

A moment in time that lasts for eternity.

Let me set the scene: a big truck, very heavy cars, construction all around. A scenario that makes any professional driver uncomfortable. It was five minutes before 11 a.m. the lunch crowd flooded the road. I was listening to a pastor from California preach on the radio. All I could do was watch the clock as my body was aching for a cigarette. I thought I would die from cramps and anxiety. Finally, I snapped, yelling and screaming at Jesus, cussing Him out. I was trying to get to Him on my own. I was trying to do it my way.

I can only remember one statement from that moment. "I am doing all this for You, and You do not want me. If I am condemned to hell, I will go there in a fireball. I can't do this. I am a failure!"

At that moment my body shook. I had no control of the vehicle. I estimate the vehicle moved about three blocks with me not in control. When I gained composure and pulled into a parking lot, I noticed a peace like I'd never experienced in my life. I clearly had seen all the trials, struggles, losses, and failures happen to prepare me for this one moment. It all happened in under two minutes. My brand-new pack of cigarettes was torn in two like they were a piece of paper. I had been released from those addictions. I WAS INTRODUCED TO CHRIST. MY CHRIST.

Daniel Farris

Daniel Farris is a self-proclaimed jack-of-all-trades and master of none. He is an optimistic person; always seeing an opportunity, not a problem. He tries very hard to listen to others with compassion because no matter how small someone's hurt seems to others; it is huge to them. Daniel enjoys his beautiful wife so very much. She is his prayer warrior and anchor. He loves active entertainment, riding bikes, motorcycles, fishing, etc. He hopes to be in Columbia working with local churches in a working retirement when the Lord blesses him and his wife.

He lives by 1 Corinthians 10:31, *Therefore, whether you eat or drink ** job family friends drive whatever*** or whatever you do. DO ALL TO THE GLORY OF GOD!* (His emphasis added)

Wrap Up

After reading these stories, now the question becomes personal. I challenge you to ask yourself, "What do these stories have to do with me?" As you look back, I am sure there are one or two stories that resonate with you more than the others. Some might have been encouraging while others might have even made you feel "a certain kind of way" about how God let the story play out. You may even be upset that God is letting a similar story in your life play out differently. The reality is, God is all knowing and He does know what is best for you and me. Through these stories, you can see His character and His love for His children. Ultimately, He wants you to seek Him, love, and trust Him. Most importantly, He wants you to call Him your Heavenly Father.

For many of us, it can be hard to love God and trust Him because of the pain and trials we have experienced. You can see this truth pointed out in many of the stories in this book. God never intended for us to live that way. He wants you to be healed and made whole; but that requires you to want that healing, give Him your broken heart, AND allow Him to work in your life.

He has given us free will which means we have the opportunity to choose what we do, who we listen to, and where we put our priorities in life. If you choose God, He will come into your life and heal every broken spot you allow Him to touch. As you have heard in many of the stories, it is a process. However, it is a process He will faithfully complete if you choose to start it and stick with it.

An important theme running through these stories is the walk here on earth is not done alone. The authors mentioned others that came along side, including counselors, mothers, fathers, spouses, daughters, grandmothers, pastors, strangers, and friends. Many times God will send someone to speak to you, be with you, or even just pray for you.

The truth is, no one is ever the same after an encounter with God. Take notice how the course of each person's life took a new direction once God met them. This change of course comes from surrendering to God. It shows up as admitting an anger towards God, seeking counseling, forgiveness , waiting, trusting God, or being ok doing things differently than the rest of the world. This step isn't always easy, but I promise you, when you choose to deepen your relationship with God, it will ALWAYS turn out good in the end!

So the question is, are you ready for God to meet you and radically change your life? He is reaching out to you right now and excited to move in miraculous ways in your life. The first step to a relationship with God is accepting the sacrifice that Jesus made for you and receiving your salvation through Jesus Christ.

Jesus said to him, "I am the way, the truth, and the life.
No one comes to the Father except through Me."
John 14:6 NKJV

Salvation: A Relationship with Jesus

You don't have to look very far to see that we live in a fallen world, one that is filled with pain, temptation, and sin. The Bible says we are all sinners and fall short of the Glory of God. (Romans 3:23) The payment for our sin is death. However, God's gift, if you choose to accept it, is eternal life in Christ Jesus. (Romans 6:23)

God so loved the world, specifically YOU, that He sent His only Son, Jesus. If you believe in your heart and confess with your mouth that you are a sinner and you need a Savior, and that Jesus came and died on the cross, was buried, and rose from the dead as payment for your sins, then you are saved! (John 3:16, Romans 10:9-10)

If you are ready to accept Jesus as your Lord and Savior, say this prayer out loud: Heavenly Father, I admit I am a sinner in need of a Savior. I believe that You sent Your Son Jesus Christ into this world as a sacrifice for my sins. I believe that He died, was buried, and on the 3rd day, He rose from the dead. I repent and turn from my sin and invite You into my heart. Jesus, I thank You for Your sacrifice and believe that You will protect me, guide me, and be with me. Amen.

Now that you have said that prayer and are saved, it is important you become connected to the Body of Christ so you can learn more about who God is, study His Word, and build a connection with other believers. Ask God to lead you, and seek a Bible-based Christian church in your area and get connected.

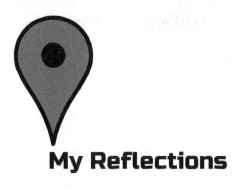

My Reflections

As was mentioned at the beginning of this book, it is no coincidence that you have this book in your hands. Each and every story was divinely authored, selected and written to touch someone who will read it. More importantly, I believe God is asking you to reflect back on times in your life where He met you. Even if you didn't know Him or believe, He was still there.

Take some quite time to reflect on your life. Ask God to show you where He met you along the way! Be bold enough to ask God the questions you hold deep in your heart. Journal your own story here.

_____

_____

_____

_____

_____

_____

_____

_____

_____

A Bit About the Bible

You may have noticed there are many references to the Bible throughout this book. If you have never really read the Bible, I would encourage you to grab a copy and read it! It's a fascinating book filled with intriguing stories of romance, betrayal, battles, victories, beheadings, and infidelity...but more importantly reconciliation, forgiveness, and love.

Some say the Bible is "Basic Instructions Before Leaving Earth." While reading and studying it, you will come to know who God is and how to live a victorious life in Him. In the Bible, Paul explained it to his student Timothy in this way:

All Scripture is given by inspiration of God, and is profitable for doctrine, for reproof, for correction, for instruction in righteousness, that the man of God may be complete, thoroughly equipped for every good work.
2 Timothy 3:16-17 NKJV

You can find a physical copy of the Bible at any bookstore and even some big box stores. In starting out, I would recommend getting the New King James Version (NKJV) or the New International Version (NIV).

You can also download one of many Bible apps on your phone. This will allow you to flip between various translations. You can also sign up for different study plans and even receive a verse of the day.

When you start reading, don't let yourself get overwhelmed. This is a life-long relationship God is calling you into!

Meeting With God

If God has met you in the pages of this book, we would love to hear about it. It is encouraging to hear how God has used our testimonies to touch the lives of others. It also gives us the opportunity to thank God and pray with you! Please visit our website or connect on social media and share with us.

🌐 www.Kingdom-Publishing.com

🅕 @Kingdom.Publish

🅞 @Kingdom.Publish

One Last Thing...

If this book has encouraged, challenged, or inspired you, please take a moment to write a review. Please visit any **online bookseller** or **GoodReads.com**, search for this book and leave a review. It would also be an honor if you share this resource on any of your social media pages.

Your review does make a difference in helping others find this resource.

Help us spread the word! Please take a pic of you and your book and post it to social media, tag Kingdom Publishing using @Kingdom.Publish and the hashtag #GodMetMeHere.

CPSIA information can be obtained
at www.ICGtesting.com
Printed in the USA
LVHW080550310822
727186LV00009B/553

9 781737 515661